Dedication

To all those who ever struggled with learning a foreign language and to Wolfgang Karfunkel

Also by Yatir Nitzany

Conversational Spanish Quick and Easy

Conversational French Quick and Easy

Conversational Italian Quick and Easy

Conversational Portuguese Quick and Easy

Conversational German Quick and Easy

Conversational Dutch Quick and Easy

Conversational Romanian Quick and Easy

Conversational Norwegian Quick and Easy

Conversational Danish Quick and Easy

Conversational Finnish Quick and Easy

Conversational Swedish Quick and Easy

Conversational Russian Quick and Easy

Conversational Ukrainian Quick and Easy

Conversational Bulgarian Quick and Easy

Conversational Polish Quick and Easy

Conversational Hebrew Quick and Easy

Conversational Yiddish Quick and Easy

Conversational Armenian Quick and Easy

Conversational Arabic Quick and Easy

Conversational Polish Quick and Easy

The Most Innovative Technique to Learn the Polish Language

YATIR NITZANY

Copyright © 2017
Yatir Nitzany
All rights reserved.
ISBN-13: 978-1951244118
ISBN-10: 146628014X
Printed in the United States of America

Foreword

About Myself

For many years I struggled to learn Spanish, and I still knew no more than about twenty words. Consequently, I was extremely frustrated. One day I stumbled upon this method as I was playing around with word combinations. Suddenly, I came to the realization that every language has a certain core group of words that are most commonly used and, simply by learning them, one could gain the ability to engage in quick and easy conversational Spanish.

I discovered which words those were, and I narrowed them down to three hundred and fifty that, once memorized, one could connect and create one's own sentences. The variations were and are *infinite*! By using this incredibly simple technique, I could converse at a proficient level and speak Spanish. Within a week, I astonished my Spanish-speaking friends with my newfound ability. The next semester I registered at my university for a Spanish language course, and I applied the same principles I had learned in that class (grammar, additional vocabulary, future and past tense, etc.) to those three hundred and fifty words I already had memorized, and immediately I felt as if I had grown wings and learned how to fly.

At the end of the semester, we took a class trip to San José, Costa Rica. I was like a fish in water, while the rest of my classmates were floundering and still struggling to converse. Throughout the following months, I again applied the same principle to other languages—French, Portuguese, Italian, and Arabic, all of which I now speak proficiently, thanks to this very simple technique.

This method is by far the fastest way to master quick and easy conversational language skills. There is no other technique that compares to my concept. It is effective, it worked for me, and it will work for you. Be consistent with my program, and you too will succeed the way I and many, many others have.

Table of Contents

Introduction to the Program 7

Introduction to the Polish Language 9

Memorization Made Easy 10

Reading and Pronunciation 11

The Program 12

Building Bridges 34

Verb Conjugation in Polish 35

Conclusion 42

Note from the Author 43

Introduction to the Program

People often dream about learning a foreign language, but usually they never do it. Some feel that they just won't be able to do it while others believe that they don't have the time. Whatever your reason is, it's time to set that aside. With my new method, you will have enough time, and you will not fail. You will actually learn how to speak the fundamentals of the language—fluently in as little as a few days. Of course, you won't speak perfect Polish at first, but you will certainly gain significant proficiency. For example, if you travel to Poland, you will almost effortlessly be able engage in basic conversational communication with the locals in the present tense and you will no longer be intimidated by culture shock. It's time to relax. Learning a language is a valuable skill that connects people of multiple cultures around the world—and you now have the tools to join them.

How does my method work? I have taken twenty-seven of the most commonly used languages in the world and distilled from them the three hundred and fifty most frequently used words in any language. This process took three years of observation and research, and during that time, I determined which words I felt were most important for this method of basic conversational communication. In that time, I chose these words in such a way that they were structurally interrelated and that, when combined, form sentences. Thus, once you succeed in memorizing these words, you will be able to combine these words and form your own sentences. The words are spread over twenty pages. In fact, there are just nine basic words that will effectively build bridges, enabling you to speak in an understandable manner (please see Building Bridges, page 34). The words will also combine easily in sentences, for example, enabling you to ask simple questions, make basic statements, and obtain a rudimentary understanding of others' communications. I have also created Memorization-Made-Easy Techniques (See page 10) for this program in order to help with the memorization of the vocabulary. Please see Reading and Pronunciation (Page 11) in order to gain proficiency in the reading and pronunciation of the Polish language prior to starting this program.

My book is mainly intended for basic present tense vocal communication, meaning anyone can easily use it to "get by" linguistically while visiting a foreign country without learning the entire language. With practice, you will be 100 percent understandable to native speakers, which is your aim. One disclaimer: this is *not* a grammar book, though it does address minute and essential grammar rules (see Basic Grammatical Requirements of the Polish Language, Page 43). Therefore, understanding complex sentences with obscure words in Polish is beyond the scope of this book.

People who have tried this method have been successful, and by the time you finish this book, you will understand and be understood in basic conversational Polish. This is the best basis to learn not only the Polish language but any language. This is an entirely revolutionary, no-fail concept, and your ability to combine the pieces of the "language puzzle" together will come with *great* ease, especially if you use this program prior to beginning a Polish class.

This is the best program that was ever designed to teach the reader how to become conversational. Other conversational programs will only teach you phrases. But this is the *only* program that will teach you how to create your *own* sentences for the purpose of becoming conversational.

The Polish Language

The official language of Poland is Polish. About 97 percent of Poland's citizens declare Polish as their native tongue, which is a very high amount of Poles that speak the language. At one point, Polish was more widespread than it is now, as Russian has overtaken the language in popularity in surrounding areas like Lithuania and Ukraine. However, Polish wasn't totally wiped out. That is, many people still know the language but don't speak it as frequently. German has greatly influenced the vocabulary of Polish, as Germany borders Poland. However, Germany isn't the only influential language. Belarus, Russia, the Czech Republic, and Slovakia all have had their fair share of influence on Polish as well.

Memorization Made Easy

There is no doubt the three hundred and fifty words in my program are the required essentials in order to engage in quick and easy basic conversation in any foreign language. However, some people may experience difficulty in the memorization. For this reason, I created Memorization Made Easy. This memorization technique will make this program so simple and fun that it's unbelievable! I have spread the words over the following twenty pages. Each page contains a vocabulary table of ten to fifteen words. Below every vocabulary box, sentences are composed from the words on the page that you have just studied. This aids greatly in memorization. Once you succeed in memorizing the first page, then proceed to the second page. Upon completion of the second page, go back to the first and review. Then proceed to the third page. After memorizing the third, go back to the first and second and repeat. And so on. As you continue, begin to combine words and create your own sentences in your head. Every time you proceed to the following page, you will notice words from the previous pages will be present in those simple sentences as well, because repetition is one of the most crucial aspects in learning any foreign language. Upon completion of your twenty pages, *congratulations,* you have absorbed the required words and gained a basic, quick-and-easy proficiency and you should now be able to create your own sentences and say anything you wish in the Polish language. This is a crash course in conversational Polish, and it works!

Reading and Pronunciation

- *A* is pronounced as the English "u" in cult.
- *Ą* is pronounced as "on" or "om" but nasalized.
- *C* is pronounced as the English "ts" in cats.
- *Ć* is pronounced similar to the English "ch."
- *CZ* is pronounced as the English "ch" in church.
- *Ch* or *kh* (read paragraph below)
- *D* is pronounced as in English, but put your tongue against the front teeth and not against the teeth ridge.
- *DZ* is pronounced as the English "ds" in beds.
- *DŻ* is pronounced as the English "j" in jam.
- *DŹ* is pronounced as the English "j" in jeep.
- *E* is pronounced as the English "e" in ten.
- *Ę* is pronounced like "en" or "em" but nasalized.
- *G* is pronounced as the English "g" in girl.
- *H* is pronounced as *kh* (please read paragraph below).
- *I* is pronounced as the English "i" in fit.
- *J* is pronounced as the English 'y' in yet.
- *Ł* is pronounced as the English 'w' in win.
- *N* is pronounced as in English, but put your tongue against the front teeth and not against the teeth ridge.
- *Ń* is pronounced as in English "ny" in canyon.
- *O* is pronounced as the English "o" in cot.
- *R* is pronounced as the Scottish or German "r": trilled by vibration of the tongue.
- *RZ* is pronounced as the English "s" in pleasure.
- *SZ* is pronounced as the English "sh" in shoes.
- *Ś* is pronounced as the "sh" in English
- *T* is pronounced as in English, but put your tongue against the front teeth and not against the teeth ridge.
- *U* is pronounced as the English "oo" in boot.
- *Ó* is pronounced as the English "oo" in boot.
- *W* is pronounced the English "v" in van.
- *Ż* is pronounced as the English "s" in pleasure.
- *Ź* is pronounced as the "si" in vision.

The Program

I / I am - Ja / Ja jestem
With you - Z tobą / z wami
With him / with her - Z nim / Z nią
For you - Dla ciebie / (Plural) dla was
Without him - Bez niego
Without them - Bez nich
Always - Zawsze
I Was – (Ja) byłem
With us - Z nami
This - To
Is - Jest
Sometimes - Czasami
Today - Dzisiaj
Are you / you are - Jesteś / ty jesteś
Better - Lepiej
You - Ty (**singular**) / wy (**plural**)
His / hers - Jego/ Jej
He, he is – On
She, she is - Ona
From – Od/ z / ze

Sentences from the vocabulary (now you can speak the sentences and connect the words)

I am with you
Ja jestem z Tobą/ Ja jestem z Wami
I am always with her
Ja jestem zawsze z nią
I am from Poland
Ja jestem z Polski
Are you from Poland?
Jesteś z Polski?/ Jesteście z Polski?
This is for you
To jest dla Ciebie/ To jest dla Was
Are you at the house?
Jesteś w domu?
Sometimes I go without him.
Czasami idę bez niego.
Are you alone today?
Czy jesteś dziś sam?

I was - Ja byłem/byłam
To be - Być
The – (see footnote)
Same - Taki sam
Good - Dobrze/ dobre
Here - Tutaj
It's / is it? - To jest/ jest?
And - I
Between - Między
Now - Teraz
Later / After - Później/ Po
If - Jeśli
Yes - Tak
Then - Wtedy
Tomorrow - Jutro
OK - Okej
Also / too / as well - Także
Day - Dzień

I was home at 5pm
W domu byłem o 17:00
Between now and tomorrow.
Między teraz a jutrem.
It's better to be home later.
Lepiej być w domu później.
If this is good, then I am happy.
Jeśli to jest dobre, to jestem szczęśliwy.
Yes, you are very good
Tak, ty jesteś bardzo dobry
I was here with them
Ja byłem tutaj z nimi
You and I.
Ty i ja.
The same day
Taki/Ten sam dzień

*In the Polish language, there are no articles such as "the" nor "a." For example, "at the house" / *w* (at) *domu* (home).

*The ending depends on the context.

*In Polish, "are you / you are" is *jesteś* / *ty jesteś*. However, the plural form is *jesteście* / *wy jesteście*.

Maybe - Może
I go - Ja pójdę
Even if - Nawet jeśli
Afterwards - Potem
Worse - Gorzej
Where - Gdzie/ Skąd
Everything - Wszystko
Somewhere - Gdzieś
What - Co/ Jaki/ Który
Almost - Prawie
There - Tam

Afterwards is worse
Potem jest gorzej

Even if I go now
Nawet jeśli ja pójdę teraz

Where is everything?
Gdzie jest wszystko?

Maybe somewhere
Może gdzieś

What? I am almost there
Co? Ja jestem prawie tam

Where are you?
Gdzie jesteś?/ Gdzie jesteście?

This is for us.
To jest dla nas.

*This *isn't* a phrase book! The purpose of this book is *solely* to provide you with the tools to create *your own* sentences!

House / home - Dom
In / at - W/ na
Car - Samochód
Already - Już
Good morning - Dzień dobry
How are you? - Jak się masz?
Where are you from? - Skąd jesteś?/ Skąd jesteście?
Me - Mnie / ja
Hello - Cześć
What is your name? - Jakie jest Twoje imię?
How old are you? - Jak stary jesteś?
Son - Syn
Daughter - Córka
Your - Twoje
Very - Bardzo
Hard - Ciężko
Still - Wciąż
Then / so - Więc

She is not in the car, so maybe she is still at the house?
Nie ma jej w samochodzie, więc może jest jeszcze w domu?
I am already in the car with your son and daughter
Ja jestem już w samochodzie z Twoim synem i córką
Good morning, how are you today?
Dzień dobry, jak się dziś czujesz?
Hello, what is your name?
Cześć, Jakie jest Twoje imię?
How old are you?
Ile masz lat?
This is very hard, but it's not impossible
To jest bardzo ciężkie, ale to nie jest niemożliwe
Where are you from?
Skąd jesteś? / Skąd jesteście?

*"Your" / *twoje* is the nominative case, while *twoim* is used to indicate the instrumental case.

Się is used as a reflexive verb, pertaining to something that somebody has to do for oneself, herself/himself, themselves, ourselves, or itself. For example, *Czy może się Pan przesunąć?* literally means "Can you move?" but can be translated as, "Can you get yourself and move?"

Thank you - Dziękuje
For – Dla/ **za** /przez
A - (no equivalent)
This is - To jest
Time - Czas
But / however – Ale/ jednak
No / not - Nie
I am not - Ja jestem nie
Away- Z dala/ nieobecny
That - Że
Similar - Podobny
Other / another - Inny
Side - Strona
Until - Do
Yesterday - Wczoraj
Without us - Bez nas
Since - Od
Evening - Wieczór
Before - Przed

Thank you, Peter.
Dziękuję, Peter.

It's almost time
To jest prawie czas

I am not here, I am far away
Nie ma mnie tutaj, jestem daleko

That house is similar to ours.
Ten dom jest podobny do naszego.

I am from the other side
Ja jestem z innej strony

But I was here until late evening
Ale ja byłem tutaj do późnego wieczoru

Since the other day
Od innego dnia

The Program

I say / I am saying - Ja mówię
What time is it? - Jaki czas jest?
I want - Ja chcę
Without you - Bez ciebie/ Bez was
Everywhere /wherever – Wszędzie/ gdziekolwiek
I go / I am going - Ja idę/ zamierzać
With - Z
My - Mój
Cousin - (M) Kuzyn, (F) Kuzynka
I need / I must - Ja potrzebuję/Ja muszę
Right now – Właśnie teraz
Night - Noc
To see - Zobaczyć /widzieć
Light - Światło
Outside - Na zewnątrz
That is/ Is that - To jest/ czy jest
During - Podczas
I see / I am seeing - Ja widzę

I am saying no / I say no
Ja mówię nie
I want to see this during the day
Ja chcę zobaczyć to podczas dnia
I see this everywhere
Ja widzę to wszędzie
I am happy without any of my cousins here
Jestem szczęśliwy bez żadnego z moich kuzynów tutaj
I need to be there at night
Ja muszę być tam w nocy
You need to be at home.
Musisz być w domu.
I see light outside
Ja widzę światło na zewnątrz
What time is it right now?
Jaki czas jest właśnie teraz?

*_Ja potrzebuję_ is used to signify "I need," while _ja muszę_ signifies "I must." However, in this program both will be used interchangeably.

*There are two forms used to express the case of "to see," and these are _zobaczyć_ and _widzieć_: **Zobaczyć** represents the perfective action / **Widzieć** represents the imperfective action. But again, this isn't a grammar book!

Conversational Polish Quick and Easy

To exchange - Wymienić
Place - Miejsce
Brother - Brat
Easy - Łatwy
To find - Znaleźć
To look for / to search - Szukać
Near - Obok, w pobliżu / blisko
Together - Razem
To sell - Sprzedać
To change - Zmienić
Of course - Oczywiście
To know - Wiedzieć / znać
To decide - Postanowić
During - Podczas
Between - Pomiędzy
Years - Lata
Two - Dwa
Late - Późno
Sky - Niebo
To - na, dla, aby, żeby (or nothing)
Up - W górę
Down - Na dół
Sorry - Przepraszam
To follow - Podążać / iść za
Her - Nią / jej
Big - Duże
New - Nowe
Never - Nigdy

This place is easy to find
To miejsce jest łatwe do znalezienia

I am saying to wait until tomorrow
Ja mówię aby poczekać do jutra

It's easy to sell this table
To jest łatwe, żeby sprzedać ten stół

I want to use this
Ja chcę użyć tego

I am never able to exchange this money at the bank.
Ja nigdy nie jestem w stanie wymienić tych pieniędzy w banku.

I want to call my brother and my dad today
Ja chcę zadzwonić do mojego brata i mojego taty dzisiaj

Where is the book?
Gdzie jest książka?

Of course I can come to the theater, and I want to sit together with you and with your sister
Oczywiście mogę przyjść do teatru i chcę siedzieć razem z tobą i twoją siostrą

I need to look for you at the mall.
Muszę szukać cię w centrum handlowym.

If you look under the table, you can see the new rug.
Jeśli zajrzysz pod stół, zobaczysz nowy dywan.

I must decide myself between both places
Ja muszę zdecydować się pomiędzy dwoma miejscami

I am sorry
Przepraszam

I need to know that everything is OK
Ja potrzebuję wiedzieć, że wszystko jest okej

I can see the sky from the window
Ja mogę widzieć niebo z okna

Is this place near?
Czy to miejsce jest blisko?

The dog wants to follow me to the store.
Pies chce iść za mną do sklepu.

*The definition of *zejść* is "to go down". However, *zejść na dół* means "to descend." In English the term "to go down" isn't commonly used; however, in other languages that term is quite prevalent.

The preposition "to" has several definitions in Polish.

Because - Ponieważ
To buy - Kupić
Both - Obie
Them / they / Their - Im/ oni / ich
Each / Every - Każdy
Book - Książka
Mine - Moja
To understand - Zrozumieć
Problem / Problems - Problem/ Problemy
I do / I am doing - Ja robię
Of - Z, na, o, ze
To look - Patrzeć
Myself – Sam, siebie, się
Enough - Wystarczająco
Food - Jedzenie
Water - Woda
Hotel - Hotel

I like this hotel because it's near the beach
Lubię ten hotel, ponieważ jest blisko plaży
I want to look at the view.
Chcę spojrzeć na widok.
I want to buy a bottle of water
Ja chcę kupić butelkę wody
Do it like this!
Zrób to tak!
That book is mine.
Ta książka jest moja.
I need to understand the problem
Ja muszę zrozumieć ten problem
From the hotel I have a view of the city
Z hotelu ja mam widok na miasto
I can work today
Ja mogę pracować dzisiaj
I do what I want.
Robię co chcę.

*To indicate "at the" or "of the," we use *na*.

*The endings of certain words vary depending on different cases. However, since this isn't a grammar book, this book won't teach you these skills.

I like - Ja lubię
There is / There are - Tam jest/ tam są
Family / Parents - Rodzina/ rodzice
Why - Dlaczego
To say - Powiedzieć
Something - Coś
To go - Chodzić /iść
Ready - Gotowy
Soon - Wkrótce
To work - Pracować
Who - Kto
Important - Ważne

I like to be at home with my parents
Ja lubię być w domu z moimi rodzicami
Why do I need to say something important?
Dlaczego muszę powiedzieć coś ważnego?
I am there with him
Ja jestem tam z nim
I am busy, but I need to be ready soon
Ja jestem zajęty, ale powinienem być gotowy wkrótce
I like to work
Ja lubię pracować
Who is there?
Kto jest tam?
I want to know if they are here.
Chcę wiedzieć, czy tu są.
I can go outside.
Mogę wyjść na zewnątrz.
There are seven dolls
Tam jest siedem lalek

*Powinienem is used to indicate "should."

*There are two forms used to indicate the verb "to go": *chodzić* and *iść*.

- *Chodzić* is used to indicate "going" but as in pattern habits. For example, when saying "I go to school every week," you would use *chodzić*.
- *Iść* is used to express "going" to a specific location. For example, when saying "I am going to the debate," you would use *iść*.

How much – Jak dużo
To take – Wziąć/skorzystać
With me - Ze mną
Instead - Zamiast
Only - Tylko
When - Kiedy
I can / Can I? - Ja mogę/ Mogę (ja)?
Or - Lub
Were - Były/ Byli
Without me - Beze mnie
Fast - Szybko
Slow - Wolno
Cold - Zimno
Inside - Wewnątrz
To eat - Jeść
Hot - Gorąco
To Drive - Jechać

How much money do I need to bring with me?
Ile pieniędzy muszę wziąć ze sobą?

I like bread instead of rice.
Lubię chleb zamiast ryżu.

Only when you can
Tylko kiedy Ty możesz

Go there without me.
Idź tam beze mnie.

I need to drive the car very fast or very slowly
Ja muszę jechać samochodem bardzo szybko lub bardzo wolno

It is cold in the library
Jest zimno w bibliotece

I like to eat a hot meal for my lunch.
Lubię zjeść ciepły posiłek na lunch.

*In regards to the conjugation of "can" for second, third, fourth person, etc., please see page 35.

To exchange - Wymienić
To answer - Odpowiedzieć
To call - Zadzwonić
Brother - Brat
Today - Dziś
To travel - Podróżwać
Delta - Delta
To learn - Nauczyć się
To sit - Siedzieć
Together - Razem
Jak - Jak
To swing - ?
To change - Zmienić
Of course - Oczywiście
To practice - Ćwiczyć
Welcome - Witam
To play - Grać
During - Podczas
To leave - Zostawić/opuścić
Many/much/a lot – Wiele/dużo
I go to - Ja idę do
Sky - Niebo
Up - ?
First - Pierwszy
W górę
Time / Times - Czas/ Czasy
Down - W dół

I need to answer many questions
Sorry - Przepraszam
Ja muszę odpowiedzieć na wiele pytań
To follow - Podążać/ iść za
I want to fly today
Her - Nią/jej
Ja chcę lecieć dziś
Big - Duże
I need to learn to swim
New - Nowa
Ja muszę nauczyć się pływać
Never - Nigdy
I want to know everything about how to play better tennis
Ja chcę wiedzieć wszystko o tym jak grać lepiej tenis
I am never able to exchange this money at the bank.
Nigdy nie jestem w stanie wymienić tych pieniędzy w banku.
Everything is about the money.
Wszystko kręci się wokół pieniędzy.
I want to call my brother and my dad today
Ja chcę zadzwonić do mojego brata i mojego taty dzisiaj
I want to leave my dog at home.
Chcę zostawić psa w domu.
Of course I can come to the theater, and I want to sit together with you and with your sister
Oczywiście ja mogę przyjść do teatru, i ja chcę siedzieć razem z tobą i twoją siostrą.
I want to travel the world
Chcę podróżować po świecie
If you look under the table, you can see the new rug.
Since the first time
Jeśli spojrzysz pod stół, zobaczysz nowy dywan.
Od pierwszego razu
I am sorry.
The children are yours
Przepraszam
I can see the sky from the window
Dzieci są Twoje
Ja mogę widzieć niebo z okna

*The dog wants to follow me to the store.
Pies chce iść za mną do sklepu

*"Exiting," while *zostawić* is used to express the action of "leaving something behind."

*The definition of *zejść* is "to go down." However, *zejść na dół* means "to descend." In English the term "to go down" isn't commonly used, however, in other languages that term is quite prevalent.

*With the knowledge you've gained so far, now try to create your own sentences!

Nobody / anyone – Nikt/ ktokolwiek
Against - Przeciwko
Us - Nas
To visit - Odwiedzić
Mom / Mother - Mama
To give - Dać
Which - Które
To meet - Spotkać
Someone - Ktoś
Just - Tylko
To walk - Chodzić
Around – Wkoło/ dookoła
Towards – W kierunku/ku
Than - Niż
Nothing / Anything - Nic

Something is better than nothing
Coś jest lepsze niż nic
I am against him
Ja jestem przeciwko niemu
We go each week to visit my family
My jedziemy każdego tygodnia aby odwiedzić moją rodzinę
I need to give you something
Ja muszę dać Ci coś
Do you want to meet someone?
Czy ty chcesz spotkać kogoś?
I am here also on Wednesdays
Ja jestem tutaj również w środy
You do this every day?
Ty robisz to codziennie?
You need to walk around the school.
Musisz przejść się po szkole.

*When asking a question, *czy* is usually placed at the beginning of the sentence to indicate the case of "do" "do we?", "do you?", "does he?" etc. However, native Polish speakers usually don't use the *czy* case (please see page 35).

Ci is the "indirect object pronoun" of the pronoun, i.e. the person who is actually affected by the action that is being carried out.

Conversational Polish Quick and Easy

To exchange - Wymienić
To call - Zadzwonić
Brother - Brat
Friend - Przyjaciel
To borrow - Pożyczyć
To look like - Wyglądać jak
Together - Razem
Grandfather - Dziadek
To change - Zmienić
To stay - Zostać
Of course - Oczywiście
Welcome - Witam
To continue - Kontynuować
During - Podczas
Way - Droga
That's why - To jest dlatego
To show - Pokazać
Sky - Niebo
To prepare - Przygotować
Up - W górę
I am not going – Ja nie będę
Down - W dół
Sorry - Przepraszam
To follow - Pokazać/Iść za
Her - Jej
Big - Duże
Near - Blisko
Never - Nigdy

Do you want to look like Arnold?
Czy chcesz wyglądać jak Arnold?
I want to borrow this book for my grandfather
Ja chcę pożyczyć tę książkę dla mojego dziadka
I want to drive and to continue on this way to my house
Ja chcę jechać i kontynuować tą drogą do mojego domu
I want to stay in Krakow because I have a friend there.
Chcę zostać w Krakowie, bo mam tam przyjaciela.
I am never able to exchange this money at the bank.
Nigdy nie jestem w stanie wymienić tych pieniędzy w banku.
I don't want to see anyone here
Nie chcę nikogo widzieć tutaj
I want to call my brother and my dad today
Ja chcę zadzwonić do mojego brata i mojego taty dzisiaj
I need to show you how to prepare breakfast
Ja muszę pokazać ci jak przygotować śniadanie
Of course I can come to the theater, and I want to sit together with you and with your sister
Oczywiście ja mogę przyjść do teatru, i ja chcę siedzieć razem z tobą i twoją siostrą.
Why don't you have the book?
Dlaczego nie ty masz książki?
If you look under the table, you can see the new rug.
That is incorrect, I don't need the car today
To jest błędne, ja nie potrzebuje samochodu dzisiaj
I am sorry.
Przepraszam
I can see the sky from the window
Ja mogę widzieć niebo z okna
The dog wants to follow me to the store.
Pies chce iść za mną do sklepu.

*Ci is the "indirect object pronoun" of the pronoun, i.e. the person who is actually affected by the action that is being carried out.
*The definition of *zejść* is "to go down." However, *zejść na dół* means "to descend." In English the term "to go down" isn't commonly used; however, in other languages that term is quite prevalent.

To remember - Pamiętać
Polish - Polskie
Number - Numer
Hour - Godzina
Dark / darkness - Ciemny /ciemność
About - O
Grandmother - Babcia
Five - Pięć
Minute / minutes - Minuta/ minuty
More - Więcej
To think - Myśleć
To do - Robić
To come - Przyjść
To hear - Posłuchać/ usłyszeć
Last - Ostatni

I need to remember your number
Ja muszę zapamiętać twój numer

This is the last hour of darkness
To jest ostatnia godzina ciemności

I want to come with you.
Chcę iść z Tobą.

I can hear my grandmother speaking Polish.
Słyszę, jak moja babcia mówi po polsku.

I need to think about this more.
Muszę o tym więcej pomyśleć.

From here to there, it's only five minutes
Stąd do tamtąd, to jest tylko pięć minu

Where is the airport
Gdzie jest lotnisko

I want to sleep
Ja chcę spaćt

To exchange - Wymienić
Again - Ponownie
Poland - Polska
To bring - Przynieść
To sit - Siedzieć
To rent - Wynajmować
Without - Bez niej
We are - My jesteśmy
To turn off - Wyłączyć
To ask - Prosić/zapytać
To stop - Zatrzymać
Permission - Pozwolenie
Early - Wcześnie
Long - Długie
Down - W dół
To follow - Podążać/Iść za
No - Nie/Jej
Big - Duży
New - Nowe
Never - Nigdy
We want to stop here
My chcemy zatrzymać się tutaj
We are from Warsaw
My jesteśmy z Warszawy
I am sorry
Przepraszam

To call - Zadzwonić
Brother - Brat
Dad - Tata
City - Miasto
Together - Razem
Which - Który
Of course - Oczywiście
Welcome - Witam
During - Podczas
Year - Rok
In - W
Sky - Niebo
Up - W górę

He must go and rent a house at the beach.
Musi iść i wynająć dom na plaży.
We are here for a long time
Jesteśmy tutaj przez długi czas
I need to turn off the lights early tonight
Ja muszę wyłączyć światła wcześnie wieczorem
I am never able to exchange this money at the bank.
Nigdy nie jestem w stanie wymienić tych pieniędzy w banku.
I want to call my brother and my dad today
Ja chcę zadzwonić do mojego brata i mojego taty dzisiaj
Of course I can come to the theater, and I want to sit together with you and with your sister
Oczywiście ja mogę przyjść do teatru, i ja chcę siedzieć razem z tobą i twoją siostrą
Your doctor is in the same building.
Twój lekarz jest w tym samym budynku.
If you look under the table, you can see the new rug.
Jeśli spojrzysz pod stół, możesz zobaczyć nowy dywan.
In order to leave, you have to ask permission.
Aby wyjść, musisz poprosić o pozwolenie.
I can see the sky from the window
Ja mogę widzieć niebo z okna
The dog wants to follow me to the store.
Pies chce iść za mną do sklepu.

*To signify "again," we use *ponownie*. However, we can use *jeszcze raz* to signify "again" as well.

*The definition of *zejść* is "to go down." However, *zejść na dół* means "to descend." In English the term "to go down" isn't commonly used; however, in other languages that term is quite prevalent.

To open - Otworzyć
To buy - Kupić
To pay - Zapłacić
Last - Ostatni
Without - Bez
Sister - Siostra
To hope - Mieć nadzieję
To live - Żyć
Nice to meet you - Miło spotkać Ciebie
Name - Imię
Last name - Nazwisko
To return - Wrócić/powrócić
Enough - Dosyć
Door - Drzwi
To get to know - Poznać
Sad - Smutne

I need to open the door for my sister
Ja muszę otworzyć drzwi dla mojej siostry
I need to buy something
Ja muszę kupić coś
I want to meet your brothers.
Chcę poznać twoich braci.
Nice to meet you, what is your name and your last name?
Miło poznać Ciebie, jakie jest twoje imię i nazwisko?
We can hope for a better future.
Możemy mieć nadzieję na lepszą przyszłość.
It is impossible to live without problems.
Nie da się żyć bez problemów.
I want to return to the United States.
Chcę wrócić do Stanów Zjednoczonych.
Why are you sad right now?
Dlaczego jesteś smutna/y teraz?

**Wrócić* literally means "to come back."

*"To return (something/someone)" is *oddać*.

*This *isn't* a phrase book! The purpose of this book is *solely* to provide you with the tools to create *your own* sentences!

To exchange - Wymieniać
To happen - Zdarzyć/stać się
To order - Zamówić
Brother - Brat
To drink - Pić
Excuse me - Wybacz mi
Child - Dziecko
Woman - Kobieta
Together - Razem
To begin/to start - Zacząć
To finish - Zakończyć
Welcome - Witam
To help - Pomóc
During - Podczas
To smoke - Palić
Years - Lata
To love - Kochać
Sky - Niebo
To talk/to speak - Rozmawiać/mówić
Up - W górę
Down - W dół
Sorry - Przepraszam
To follow - Podążać/iść za
Her - Nią/Jej
Big - Duże
New - Nowe
Never - Nigdy

This must happen today
To musi się zdarzyć dziś

Excuse me, my child is here as well
Wybacz mi, moje dziecko jest tutaj również

I want to order a soup.
Chcę zamówić zupę.

We want to start the class soon.
Chcemy wkrótce rozpocząć zajęcia.

I am never able to exchange this money at the bank.
Nigdy nie jestem w stanie wymienić tych pieniędzy w banku.

In order to finish at three o'clock this afternoon, I need to finish soon
Aby skończyć o trzeciej po południu, muszę skończyć wcześniej.

I want to call my brother and my dad today
Ja chcę zadzwonić do mojego brata i mojego taty dzisiaj

I want to learn how to speak perfect Polish.
Ja chcę nauczyć się mówić perfekcyjnie po polsku.

Of course I can come to the theater, and I want to sit together with you and your sister
Oczywiście ja mogę przyjść do teatru, i ja chcę siedzieć razem z tobą i twoją siostrą

I don't want to smoke again
Ja nie chcę palić ponownie

If you look under the table, you can see the new rug.
Jeśli zajrzysz pod stół, zobaczysz nowy dywan.

I need you.
Ja potrzebuję cię

I am sorry.
Ja przepraszam cię

I can see the sky from the window
Ja mogę widzieć niebo z okna

I love you.
Ja kocham cię

The dog wants to follow me to the store.
Pies chce iść za mną do sklepu.

I see you
Ja widzę cię

I want to help
Ja chcę pomóc

The definition of *zejść* is "to go down." However, *zejść na dół* means "to descend." In English the term "to go down" isn't commonly used; however, in other languages that term is quite prevalent.

To read - Czytać/przeczytać
To write - Pisać
To teach - Uczyć
To close - Zamknąć
To turn on - Włączyć
To prefer - Woleć
To put - Położyć
Less - Mniej
Sun - Słońce
Month - Miesiąc
I talk – Rozmawiać/ Mówić
Exact – Dokładnie/wiernie
To choose - Wybrać
To allow - Pozwolić/umożliwić
Man – Człowiek / mężczyzna

I need this book to learn how to read and write in Polish.
Potrzebuję tej książki, aby nauczyć się czytać i pisać po polsku.
I want to teach English in Poland.
Chcę uczyć angielskiego w Polsce.
I want turn on the lights and close the door.
Chcę zapalić światło i zamknąć drzwi.
I want to pay less than you.
Chcę płacić mniej niż ty.
I prefer to put this here.
Wolę umieścić to tutaj.
I speak with the boy and the girl in Russian
Ja rozmawiam z chłopcem i dziewczyną po rosyjsku
There is sun outside today.
Na ulicy dzisiaj jest słońce.
Is it possible to know the exact date?
Czy to możliwe, aby znać dokładną datę?
I need to allow him to go with us.
Muszę pozwolić mu iść z nami.
He is a different man now.
Jest teraz innym człowiekiem.

*Pozwolić means "to allow," while umożliwić means "to permit."

*"Man" is człowiekiem; however mężczyzna can be used to signify a "man," as well.

*With the knowledge you've gained so far, now try to create your own sentences!

To exchange - Wymiana
To call - Zadzwonić
Brother - Brat
Dad - Tata
To sit - Siedzieć
Together - Razem
To change - Zmienić
Of course - Oczywiście
Welcome - Witam
During - Podczas
Years - Lata
Sky - Niebo
Up - W górę

Down - W dół
Sorry - Przepraszam
To follow – Podążać/ Iść za
Her - Nią/ Jej
Big - Duże
New - Nowe
Never - Nigdy

I am never able to exchange this money at the bank.
Nigdy nie jestem w stanie wymienić tych pieniędzy w banku.

I want to call my brother and my dad today
Ja chcę zadzwonić do mojego brata i mojego taty dzisiaj

Of course I can come to the theater, and I want to sit together with you and with your sister
Oczywiście ja mogę przyjść do teatru, i ja chcę siedzieć razem z tobą i twoją siostrą

If you look under the table, you can see the new rug.
Jeśli zajrzysz pod stół, zobaczysz nowy dywan.

I am sorry.
Przepraszam

I can see the sky from the window
Ja mogę widzieć niebo z okna

The dog wants to follow me to the store.
Pies chce iść za mną do sklepu.

*The definition of *zejść* is "to go down." However, *zejść na dół* means "to descend." In English the term "to go down" isn't commonly used; however, in other languages that term is quite prevalent.

To believe - Wierzyć
Morning - Rano
Except - Wyjątek/poza
To promise - Obiecać
Good night - Dobranoc
To recognize – Rozpoznać/uznać
People - Ludzie
To move - Przenieść
Far - Daleko
Different - Różne, inne
Quickly - Szybko
To receive - Otrzymać
Throughout - Przez
Tonight - Dziś wieczorem
Through - Poprzez
Him / his - Go / jego
Our - Nasz
On - Na

I believe everything except for this
Ja wierzę, we wszystko, z wyjątkiem tego
Come here quickly.
Chodź tu szybko.
I can't recognize him.
Nie mogę go rozpoznać.
I see the sun in the morning from the kitchen
Ja widzę słońce rano z kuchni
I want his car
Ja chcę ten samochód
The plant is on our table
Roślina jest na naszym stole
Our house is on the mountain.
Nasz dom jest na górze.
I go into the house from the front entrance and not through the yard.
Wchodzę do domu przednim wejściem, a nie przez podwórze.
I want a car before the next year
Ja chcę samochód przed następnym rokiem

*There are two forms used to express "next," *blisko* and *następny*. **Blisko/niedaleko** means "next to," "near," or "close." **Następny** is used to express "the next," or "the following."

Różne means "different," while *innym* means "another."

To exchange - Wymienić
To wish - Życzyć
To call - Zadzwonić
Bad - Zły
Brother - Brat
To get - Uzyskać
Dad - Tata
To forget - Zapomnieć
Everybody/everyone – Wszyscy/ każdy
Past - Przeszłość
Altogether - Razem
Of course - Oczywiście
To feel - Czuć
To change - Zmienić
Wonderful - Wspaniały
Next - Następny
Welcome - Witamy
Close - Blisko
To like - Lubić
During - Podczas
Years - Lata
Sky - Niebo
In front – Z przodu
Person - Osoba
Up - W górę
Behind - Za
Well - Cóż
Down - W dół
Restaurant - Restauracja
Sorry - Przepraszam
Bathroom - Łazienka
Party - Część
To follow - Podążać/ Iść za
Goodbye - Żegnaj
Her - Nią/ Jej
Big - Duże
New - Nowe
Never - Nigdy

I don't want to wish anything bad
Ja nie chcę życzyć niczego złego
I must forget everybody from my past
Ja muszę zapomnieć wszystkich z mojej przeszłości.
I am never able to exchange this money at the bank.
Nigdy nie jestem w stanie wymienić tych pieniędzy w banku.
I want to call my brother and my dad today
Ja chcę zadzwonić do mojego brata i mojego taty dzisiaj
Of course I can come to the theater, and I want to sit together with you and with your sister
Oczywiście ja mogę przyjść do teatru, i ja chcę siedzieć razem z tobą i twoją siostrą.
If you look under the table, you can see the new rug.
Jeśli zajrzysz pod stół, zobaczysz nowy dywan.
Which is the best restaurant in the area?
Która restauracja jest najlepszą w okolicy?
I can see the sky from the window
Ja mogę widzieć niebo z okna
I can feel the heat.
Czuję ciepło.
The dog wants to follow me to the store.
Pies chce iść za mną do sklepu.
I need to repair a part of the cabinet of the bathroom.
Muszę naprawić część szafki w łazience.
I like the house, but it is very small.
Podoba mi się ten dom, ale jest bardzo mały.

*The definition of *zejść* is "to go down." However, *zejść na dół* means "to descend." In English the term "to go down" isn't commonly used; however, in other languages that term is quite prevalent.

Tobą is the dative form of "you."

To remove - Usunąć
Please - Proszę
Beautiful - Piękne
To lift - Podnieść
Include / including - Zawiera
Belong - Należeć
To hold - Trzymać
To check - Sprawdzić
Small - Mały
Real - Prawdziwy
Week - Tydzień
Size - Rozmiar
Even though - Nawet jeśli
Doesn't - Nie
So - Tak (is used to express "so big," "so small," or "so fast."),
So - Więc (as in "then")
Price - Cena

She wants to remove this door, please
Ona chce usunąć te drzwi, proszę
This doesn't belong here, I need to check again
To nie należy tutaj, ja muszę to sprawdzić jeszcze raz
This week the weather was very beautiful
W tym tygodniu pogoda była bardzo piękna
Is that a real diamond?
Czy to prawdziwy diament?
We need to check the size of the house
Musimy sprawdzić rozmiar domu
I want to lift this.
Chcę to podnieść.
The sun is high in the sky.
Słońce jest wysoko na niebie.
Can you please put the wood in the fire?
Czy możesz dołożyć drewno do ognia?
Can you please hold my hand?
Czy możesz proszę potrzymać mnie za rękę?
I can pay this although the price is expensive
Ja mogę zapłacić to chociaż cena jest droga

*Była is used to express "was."

*Jak duży jest dom literally means "how big is the house."

Building Bridges

In Building Bridges, we take six conjugated verbs that have been selected after studies I have conducted for several months in order to determine which verbs are most commonly conjugated, and which are then automatically followed by an infinitive verb. For example, once you know how to say, "I need," "I want," "I can," and "I like," you will be able to connect words and say almost anything you want more correctly and understandably. The following three pages contain these six conjugated verbs in first, second, third, fourth, and fifth person, as well as some sample sentences. Please master the entire program up until here prior to venturing onto this section.

I want - Chcę
I need - Potrzebuję
I can - Mogę
I like - Lubię
I go - Idę
I have - Mam
I must/I have to - Muszę

I want to go to my apartment
Ja chcę iść do mojego mieszkania
I can go with you to the bus station
Ja mogę iść z tobą na dworzec autobusowy
I need to leave the museum.
Muszę opuścić muzeum.
I like to eat oranges.
Lubię jeść pomarańcze.
I am going to teach a class
Ja zamierzam uczyć klasę
I have to speak to my teacher
Ja muszę porozmawiać z moim nauczycielem

Please master *every* single page up until here prior to attempting the following two pages!

You want - Ty chcesz/ Wy chcecie
Do you want? - Czy ty chcesz? / Czy wy chcecie?
He wants / does he want - On chce/ Czy on chce?
She wants / does she want - Ona chce /Czy ona chce?
We want / do we want - My chcemy /Czy my chcemy?
They want / do they want - Oni chcą /Czy oni chcą?
You (plural) want? - Wy chcecie/ Czy wy chcecie?

You need - Ty potrzebujesz/ Wy potrzebujecie
Do you need? - Czy ty potrzebujesz? / Czy wy potrzebujecie?
He needs / does he need - On potrzebuje / Czy on potrzebuje?
She needs / does she need - Ona potrzebuje /Czy ona potrzebuje?
We need / do we need - My potrzebujemy / Czy my potrzebujemy?
They need / do they need - Oni potrzebują /Czy oni potrzebują?
You (plural) need - Wy potrzebujecie/ Czy wy potrzebujecie?

You can - Ty możesz/ Wy możecie
Can you? - Czy ty możesz? / Czy wy możecie?
He can / can he - On może / Czy on może?
She can / can she - Ona może / Czy ona może?
We can / can we - My możemy / czy my możemy?
They can / can they - Oni mogą / Czy oni mogą?
You (plural) want - Wy checie/ czy wy chcecie?

You like - Ty Lubisz/ Wy idziecie
Do you like? - Czy Ty Lubisz? / Czy wy lubicie?
He likes / does he like - On lubi /Czy on lubi?
She likes / does she like - Ona lubi / Czy ona lubi?
We like / do we like - My lubimy /Czy my lubimy?
They like / do they like - Oni lubią /Czy oni lubią?
You (plural) like - Wy lubicie/ Czy wy lubicie?

You go – Ty Idziesz/ Wy Idziecie
Do you go? - Czy idziesz? / Czy idziecie?
He goes / does he go - On idzie /Czy on idzie?
She goes / does she go - Ona idzie /Czy ona idzie?
We go / do we go - My idziemy /Czy my idziemy?
They go / do they go - Oni idą /Czy oni idą?
You (plural) go - Wy idziecie/ Czy wy idziecie?

You have - Ty masz/ Wy macie
Do you have? - Czy ty masz? / Czy wy macie?
He has / does he have - On ma /Czy on ma?
She has / does she have - Ona ma/Czy ona ma?
We have / do we have - My mamy/Czy my mamy?
They have / do they have - Oni mają /Czy oni mają?
You (plural) have - Wy macie/ Czy wy macie?

You must - Ty musisz/ Wy musicie
Must you? - Czy ty musisz?/ Czy wy musicie?
He must/ must he? - On musi / Czy on musi?
She must/ must she? - Ona musi/Czy Ona musi?
We must/ must we? - My musimy/Czy my musimy?
They must/ must they? - Oni muszą / Czy oni muszą?
You (plural) must? - Wy muście / Czy wy muście?

Do you want to go?
Czy ty chcesz iść?

Does he want to fly?
Czy on chce lecieć?

We want to swim
My chcemy pływać

Do they want to run?
Czy oni chcą biegać?

Do you need to clean?
Czy ty potrzebujesz posprzątać?

She needs to sing a song
Ona potrzebuje zaśpiewać piosenkę

We need to travel
My potrzebujemy podróżować

They don't need to fight
Oni nie muszą walczyć

You (plural) need to save your money.
Wy musicie oszczędzać pieniądze.

Can you hear me?
Czy ty słyszysz mnie?

He can dance very well
On potrafi tańczyć bardzo dobrze

We can go out tonight
Możemy wyjść dziś wieczorem

The fireman can break the door during an emergency.
Strażak może wyłamać drzwi w sytuacji awaryjnej.

Do you like to eat here?
Czy ty lubisz jeść tutaj?

He likes to spend time here
On lubi spędzać czas tutaj

We like to fix the house
My lubimy naprawiać ten dom

They like to cook
Oni lubią gotować

You (plural) like to play soccer.
Wy lubicie grać w piłkę nożną.

Do you go to the movies on weekends?
Czy chodzisz do kina w weekendy?

He goes fishing
On idzie łowić ryby

We are going to relax
My zamierzamy się zrelaksować

They go out to eat at a restaurant everyday.
Codziennie wychodzą coś zjeść do restauracji.

Do you have money?
Czy ty masz pieniądze?

He must go to sleep
On musi iść spać

She must look outside
Ona musi patrzeć na zewnątrz

We have to sign our names
My musimy podpisać nasze imiona

They have to send the letter
Oni muszą wysłać list

You (plural) have to stand in line.
Wy musicie stać w kolejce.

Other Useful Tools in the Polish Language

Days of the Week
Sunday - Niedziela
Monday - Poniedziałek
Tuesday - Wtorek
Wednesday - Środa
Thursday - Czwartek
Friday - Piątek
Saturday - Sobota

Months
January - Styczeń
February - Luty
March - Marzec
April - Kwiecień
May - Maj
June - Czerwiec
July - Lipiec
August - Sierpień
September - Wrzesień
October - Październik
November - Listopad
December - Grudzień

Seasons
Spring - Wiosna
Summer - Lato
Autumn - Jesień
Winter - Zima

Cardinal Directions
North - Północ
South - Południe
East - Wschód
West – Zachód

Colors
Black - Czarny
White - Biały

Gray - Szary
Red - Czerwony
Blue - Niebieski
Yellow - Żółty
Green - Zielony
Orange - Pomarańczowy
Purple - Fioletowy
Brown - Brązowy

Numbers
One - Jeden
Two - Dwa
Three - Trzy
Four - Cztery
Five - Pięć
Six - Sześć
Seven - Siedem
Eight - Osiem
Nine - Dziewięć
Ten - Dziesięć
Eleven - Jedenaście
Twelve - Dwanaście
Thirteen - Trzynaście
Fourteen - Czternaście
Fifteen - Piętnaście
Sixteen - Szesnaście
Seventeen - Siedemnaście
Eighteen - Osiemnaście
Nineteen - Dziewiętnaście
Twenty - Dwadzieścia
Thirty - Trzydzieści
Forty - Czterdzieści
Fifty - Pięćdziesiąt
Sixty - Sześćdziesiąt
Seventy - Siedemdziesiąt
Eighty - Osiemdziesiąt
Ninety - Dziewięćdziesiąt
One hundred - Sto
Thousand - Tysiąc
Million - Milion
Billion - Miliard

Congratulations! Now You Are on Your Own!

If you merely absorb the required three hundred and fifty words in this book, you will then have acquired the basis to become conversational in Polish! After memorizing these three hundred and fifty words, this conversational foundational basis that you have just gained will trigger your ability to make improvements in conversational fluency at an amazing speed! However, in order to engage in quick and easy conversational communication, you need a special type of basics, and this book will provide you with just that.

Unlike the foreign language learning systems presently used in schools and universities, along with books and programs that are available on the market today, that focus on *everything* but being conversational, *this* method's sole focus is on becoming conversational in Polish as well as any other language. Once you have successfully mastered the required words in this book, there are two techniques that if combined with these essential words, can further enhance your skills and will result in you improving your proficiency tenfold. *However*, these two techniques will only succeed *if* you have completely and successfully absorbed the three hundred and fifty words. *After* you establish the basis for fluent communications by memorizing these words, you can enhance your conversational abilities even more if you use the following two techniques.

The first step is to attend a Polish language class that will enable you to sharpen your grammar. You will gain additional vocabulary and learn past and present tenses, and if you apply these skills that you learn in the class, together with the three hundred and fifty words that you have previously memorized, you will be improving your conversational skills tenfold. You will notice that, conversationally, you will succeed at a much higher rate than any of your classmates. A simple second technique is to choose Polish subtitles while watching a movie. If you have successfully mastered and grasped these three hundred and fifty words, then the combination of the two—those words along with the subtitles—will aid you considerably in putting all the grammar into perspective, and again, conversationally, you will improve tenfold.

Once you have established a basis of quick and easy conversation in Polish with those words that you just attained, every additional word or grammar rule you pick up from there on will be gravy. And these additional words or grammar rules can be combined with the three hundred and fifty words, enriching your conversational abilities even more. Basically, after the research and studies I've conducted with my method over the years, I came to the conclusion that in order to become conversational, you first must learn the words and *then* learn the grammar.

The Polish language is compatible with the mirror translation technique. Likewise, with *this* language, you can use this mirror translation technique in order to become conversational, enabling you to communicate even more effortlessly. Mirror translation is the method of translating a phrase or sentence, word for word from English to Polish, by using these imperative words that you have acquired through this program (such as the sentences I used in this book). Latin languages, Middle Eastern languages, and Slavic languages, along with a few others, are also compatible with the mirror translation technique. Though you won't be speaking perfectly proper and precise Polish, you will still be fully understood and, conversation-wise, be able to get by just fine.

Conclusion

Congratulations! You have completed all the tools needed to master the Polish language, and I hope that this has been a valuable learning experience. Now you have sufficient communication skills to be confident enough to embark on a visit to Poland, impress your friends, and boost your resume so *good luck*.

This program is available in other languages as well, and it is my fervent hope that my language learning programs will be used for good, enabling people from all corners of the globe and from all cultures and religions to be able to communicate harmoniously. After memorizing the required three hundred and fifty words, please perform a daily five-minute exercise by creating sentences in your head using these words. This simple exercise will help you grasp conversational communications even more effectively. Also, once you memorize the vocabulary on each page, follow it by using a notecard to cover the words you have just memorized and test yourself and follow *that* by going back and using this same notecard technique on the pages you studied during the previous days. This repetition technique will assist you in mastering these words in order to provide you with the tools to create your own sentences.

Every day, use this notecard technique on the words that you have just studied.

Everything in life has a catch. The catch here is just consistency. If you just open the book, and after the first few pages of studying the program, you put it down, then you will not gain anything. However, if you consistently dedicate a half hour daily to studying, as well as reviewing what you have learned from previous days, then you will quickly realize why this method is the most effective technique ever created to become conversational in a foreign language. My technique works! For anyone who doubts this technique, all I can say is that it has worked for me and hundreds of others.

NOTE FROM THE AUTHOR

Thank you for your interest in my work. I encourage you to share your overall experience of this book by posting a review. Your review can make a difference! Please feel free to describe how you benefited from my method or provide creative feedback on how I can improve this program. I am constantly seeking ways to enhance the quality of this product, based on personal testimonials and suggestions from individuals like you.

Thanks and best of luck,\
Yatir Nitzany

www.ingramcontent.com/pod-product-compliance
Lightning Source LLC
Chambersburg PA
CBHW052107110526
44591CB00013B/2383